Nerve Language

Nerve Language

Brian Henderson

PEDLAR PRESS | TORONTO

ACKNOWLEDGEMENTS
The publisher wishes to thank the Canada Council for the Arts and the Ontario Arts Council for their generous support of our publishing program.

LIBRARY AND ARCHIVES CANADA
CATALOGUING IN PUBLICATION

Henderson, Brian, 1948-

    Nerve language / Brian Henderson. – 1st ed.

Poems.

ISBN 978-1-897141-13-7

    1. Schreber, Daniel Paul, 1842-1911–Poetry. I. Title.

PS8565.E5IN47 2007   C811'.54
    C2006-906929-8

First Edition

EDITED FOR THE PRESS Don McKay
COVER ART Joan Kaufman
DESIGN Zab Design & Typography, Winnipeg

Printed in Canada

In Memoriam Ruth Doris Henderson (1922–2006)

Contents

The Fleetingly Improvised

The Harrowing of the Planets

The Drug Vehicle

The Coming-Through-the-Mirror Thought

God's Tintinnabulation

The Acceleration of the Rays

At the Persian Café

The Nerve Contact

The Glistering of Female Nerves

Nearing the Home Near the Woods

The Content of Saturation

Every body experiences everything that goes on in the universe, so much so that he who sees everything might read in any body what is happening anywhere, and even what has happened or will happen.

—LEIBNIZ

He searched for words and they came tumbling out, but it was torture.

—JACOB LENZ

We will first turn to other languages. But the dictionaries that we consult tell us nothing new, perhaps only because we ourselves speak a language that is foreign.

—FREUD

Initiates into the tradition of the ancestors can be recruited in several ways....Individuals who have suffered severe cases of soul loss...may have to take on some of the burden of the tradition in order to alleviate their own maladies.

—TIMOTHY J. KNAB

The Fleetingly Improvised

Phantom Mind

How to say not climbing into the bodies of the dead.
How to not cry out in the night.
How to avoid the soiling.
How to know something.
The fond kiss where there was none.
No one to say it.
What would invite itself.
How not to complete a sentence while completing it.
How to complete this knot while untying it.
Sentencing. So it might not be possible.
Not have happened.

Self Portrait with Nerves

Colour of skin, nearly blue   *Rivering through cities, nerves are hot lava*
Long, narrow, now shaven, face   *Nerves the roots of the tree*
                                Inventing thirst
How does one get used
To this state of affairs   *Nerves the cracked mirror*
I walk as though I were catching myself
From falling   *The rhizomes of stars*
I stand as though bones held sway
Not sinew, muscle or nerves   *The lines that bind you to the sentence are*
                                    Nerves
I grow a writing callus
And have stopped making judgements   *God's language of reversal*
                    In which poison is food, and juice venom
                         Tunes the Nerve Language
And I am telling you all this
While you are imagining
Something else

Gathering Strangeness

Reading a line in Rumi I catch a glimpse
of another life lived—
the house with the giant linden trees,
the rain-filled night on the balcony.
A moment of being two places at once.
I re-read the line
and it is gone. What rain-filled night?
Pasts that shimmer over objects in the room
like something made of heat and sky are whose?

Evening imperceptibly darkens
as if it were thinking about thunder
and the descending sunlight
that had opened a brief door in the kitchen wall
has closed it.
Dervish, I read, means doorway.
Entering a room, or a memory, or a life,
perhaps as others are leaving, or after they have left.
In a dream, not being able to get back in the way I'd come.

Out in the garden, everything that was once familiar
is left to gather its truth in the rain,
strangeness soaking into everything.

The house sailing in mind circles
Refracts an architecture of underglimmer
Penetralium harbouring the lived through
In their nooks, returners like the snake know
The fragile moment of the letter
That calls out your name
And would claim you
Air chilled by early morning hail
Tiny volute not forgotten in the basement drawer
But secreted
Every turn mortgaged to love
Sudden clairvoyance.

The Miracle of Unmanning

From then on my wife's visits ceased.
Only once at the window I recognized her
as one of the fleetingly
improvised. The photo on her dresser:
that of the doctor. It was they
held me down with voluptuousness,
the female nerves, starting to enter my body
my ever-increasing nervousness
attracting God's attention
becoming danger, abandoned
on the floor
and dragged out of bed in the darkness of night
to a cell, force-fed,
transformed, given over, and no one seems to have known

what was to happen
to such a forsaken human being.

Sparta of Childhood

Eyes the colour of leather, the colour
of wood, famous for intricate equipment
of children's discipline we wore
like clothes—a beetle's armour—and treatises
on moral education, late
in life, after a first son's suicide, he
walked into despair
as if into a river,
leaving us on the shore, tip
of the straightening board brushing my groin
again those punishment contraptions blooming
branches of sperms and scissors
come into me like stripping a green twig, a
refusal to howl
now that pieces of souls are splinters in me
a discipline memorizing me
to the heartwood.

The Harrowing of the Planets

Innocence Is the Weakest Defence

Rippled and dazzled in the waking light
wind frisking each needle of the pine forest
the room's objects that were once here
think they are drowned for a moment
before recollecting and composing themselves
somewhere else. Of course they are being
molested by glances: they've all been removed
against their will—

Don't look, but surround yourself with looking—

And so they want to take everything from me,
my shoes, my wife, my sanity, my position, and
so my dreams, writing instruments, shirts and
cuff links, my chess pieces, books,
toiletries, handkerchiefs, and so the
reputation of my father, and so
called mad, I am otherwise entirely,
called paranoid—rather the apotheosis
of these vanished things which made up who I was,
my stillborn children, the crushing bundles of spears of light,
I am what's left over, hunger of dispersal

Something terrible has happened.
I'm looking out the window
into the grey fog of dawn
and can see only the line of young maples
behind the wall. They have
burst into flame.
Those entrusted with our lives
have used some weapon such that
only shells of things remain,
and I, the last person on earth
shiver in the window
where light has gone astray.

Sabine

I did not expect to see you
like this.
     You look at me
with an insect look.
     You think I've slept
with someone else.
     The doctor has cured me
while you've been inside.
     If I go
to Switzerland now,
I will have been already.
     It's because I need the money
you will not sign
the cheques for.
     I cannot have you
home.
     It is a spider
with ray-like legs.
     I cannot have you home.

Night and Day

All along the golden light of evening,
the Danaids of voices—to be constantly demanded
to complete the sentences
unendurable, unendurable
this perverse prosthesis of mind I cannot sleep
let me imagine you not
in another country think
rather of the winged vertebrae those
angels of history who are afraid
to take their eyes off the past emerging
from their graves like night-flying moths
being released from what they were, perhaps
bone is merely larval and I could wake to human language
your sleeping breath softly in my ear

Voluptuousness is a state of mind
the hands of their souls
inside me
has since run like a red thread
through my entire life
that God does not really understand
the living human being
because He deals only with corpses and souls
in order to draw up their nerves
and completely misunderstands
the needs of an actually living
human body
and treats me like a soul
sometimes like a corpse
and thinks He can force upon me
the soul's mode of thinking and
feeling, its language, etc
and demand from me continual
voluptuousness, continual
thinking

trying to think with some clarity, surrounded by
the gods of the asylum, the starched attendants, the
lingoed doctors, the patients at the pinnacle of abject
longing, the rays crashing into my skull, burning up,
or turning to lightning, my little tree of veins, a river
system in ice as seen from high above as if you were a
visitor from another planet making an entrance for
the first time. What on earth would you say? Who are
these extraordinary figures in linen overalls covered in
soot, their heads becoming beetle heads or bird heads
at random? How time does not take us with it, but
maroons us sometimes. I'm certain, since this morning,
a huge gap has opened and I've been catapulted or cut
off in a future—a watch might have been of some help,
but they've taken it from me. Is it possible to go back, to
where, no matter what, everything, even just from the
outside, appears as before? Even for a minute?

The Drug Vehicle

Reading Thoughts

The writing-down-system trying to exhaust
me down to the last thought
by detailing everything, the colour
of the bed covers, the angle of the rays,
the wood of the shutters, the sharp bites of stars,
the feel of the polish on the table in the corner,
and when there is such a thing as a peaceful moment
suddenly up flies such nonsense to clutter it up,
the word *wretch* frequently scribbled,
disparity of God, if only the cursed
play-with-human-beings would cease
endlessly into the discipline-contraption of the night.

Searching for the Golden Drop

If in a cell furnished for maniacal patients:
iron bedstead, bedpan, some bedding,
and most of the time they were blacked out
by heavy wooden shutters, without light
or matches, or any object
which could be used for some occupation,
clad, in the darkened cell, only in a shirt,
barefoot in the chill, —even my slippers
had been taken from me,
I tied knots in the four corners of my handkerchief
and untied them again, partly in bed
and partly while walking around
trying to recall aloud some memories of my life,
screwing with God, His hard
forsaken moment of truth
would climb out of the bed
and distance itself from me.

Sleep at night
mostly poor, moans
stands in bed, stands rigidly
in front of the window with eyes closed
an expression of listening on his face.
Called back. The instant
nerve contact, you'd know it,
the total mental individuality
of a human being in every fleeting filament
and the forsaken, shadow people
drifting in and out of my body

The Play-with-Human-Beings

They accuse me of breaking
the strings, but it's impossible,
the hammers only strike the strings
no matter how hard the keys are themselves
struck. You try it.
                    How do you tell
when there is a crisis in God's realm?
We live in a network of nerves
where the universe is inscribed
in every single string.
I honestly long only
for sleep's quiet current
but I am damaged by miracles,
the spontaneously generated insects,
the tears in my skin, my internal organs
pulled this way and that,
the constant sounds of weeping.
Do not be mistaken, the phenomenon
of the talking birds is marvellous and like
a fairytale, and I am learning all the time
how to be cured,
or how the broken
can be beautiful-
ly, unbroken-
ly played.

Seelenpolitik

Imagine your soul flowing out of you, the feeling of a string being pulled through the back of your head, Troy precipitating out of myth treasure by treasure into the real, flowing out of you backwards, out of your shithole like memory flowing backwards, the occasional exposé of a false medium in the papers.

I would like to ask under what circumstances a person considered insane can be detained in an asylum against their express will?

Imagine an innocuous four-petalled flower in which the map of the whole of the underworld shimmers, its witchy music's fragrance. Imagine the doctors believe this not to be a map, but a sign that only means madness. (Jung and Freud have yet to read the text.) And your fine forensic points gleam like fireflies on a June night.

The greatest miracle of all would be walking through those crumbling gates, walking with your daughter in the hills green with stillness.

If real life is not noted for its realism, what do you think your life is? And to whom might I be speaking?

No such thing as speaking here, not a word
in that language, only the splashy noises
at the end of the pen, recalling the silences
of reading my father's books: the Greek body,
the sandclock of obedience for children.

The stars are bigger than they were then,
frost apples
                        among which the doctor's soul
flies, looking for its victim.

At the solstice of sanity
fear takes prisoners. There are no
words for it, how they
do it in their language,
dementia, madness, wretch, ruin;
understanding not one of their words,
not a word,
no such thing.

The Coming-Through-the-Mirror Thought

A Short History of Sonnenstein

The idea of the cure. It strikes one as grandiose, if not merely optimistic. And on whose behalf is a lurking and unmentioned question. But leave it to the French; it was a French idea: to separate the crazy from the criminal, and not simply inter them together.

And so Sonnenstein was blessed. It shed its old skin as prison for felons and madmen and in 1811 became an asylum for the acutely insane. Gardens were worked, and in the many artisanal shops many things were made; prayer in the chapel; musical and theatrical performances. And thus the cure rate was rather a showcase.

But by the time I arrived, the asylum had been forced to accept the truly nasty crazies, the chronically insane, the screamers, the violent, the recalcitrant, those who drooled and ate their own stool, and there was simply not enough money.

Nonetheless, in 1911, there occurred a festive centennial, altars bedecked with flowers, speeches from ministerial dignitaries celebrating the castle's origins as a Roman castrum, its naming in 1409 by Wilhelm the One-Eyed, ladies in feathers, men with cigars. One might ask where the mad were.

On the long history of institutions glory always seems to darken. Sonnenstein can still be seen today in all its gloomy grandeur. There is a rather large plaque on what is now Sonnenstein Vocational School: *In memory of the victims of fascist crimes committed in the former asylum for acute and chronic patients 1940–41*. It carefully avoids mentioning the final continuation: Nazi euthanasia and the testing of Zyclon B.

Representations

Take an image and
lock it in the drawer
for which there is no key.
We see the volute of the wound
as the furled extract of the event
that caused it.
                      Is the tincture
the plant, the portrait, the person?
Essential slipping, in a sense
innocence offered, the pain
of this something
                             of me
(in the thinking prison)

You are to be represented as denying God,
as being stupid, as being excessively voluptuous.

Why not. Why,
                      if. Why,
because I.
                Lacking now is.
Who says,
            God does not wish to dissolve in you?

Each one, a word
looking for its sentence. *Fall* light
sifting through pine
into this empty drawer.

Picturing

It's demanded of me to relate to myself everything that happens. I don't want to know any of it. How to escape it? Why can't I just let it happen? Why not just say what they want me to say?

I am given peace only by sewing, dusting, gardening, playing at the piano. And when doing these things I picture myself before the mirror actually in the other room dressed as a woman. The greatest feeling of well-being is achieved at night when I easily imagine female sexual pleasure, and I am filled with the flower of female nerves, the swan of bed-clothing, a golden serum of dawn.

Loud Thinking

Like curious gold fish the rays approach me, but any human noise near me scatters them and then God withdraws to an excessive distance, tearing off a piece of my skull as if it were evidence.

In my room, or in the garden if I am turned toward God (in the pacing of my thinking) everything grows deathly quiet and God has no wish to withdraw. I feel as if I were moving among walking corpses. (And so I must to continue to think—too much unbearable thinking— over the unwelcome unmatched sounds of the world climbing the scales of injustice.)

Listening

Yes, God is listening, listening to the world
He is listening to the world through me,
my ears bleed with listening.
I can hear the mosquito
spitting its juice beneath my skin,
and the morning air thinking about stirring.
Each word spoken across the room
is a thunderclap
a blow on the head.
Luckily, the voices of the birds whisper,
whisper that I am not merely a specimen,
but even though He may hear this,
I doubt He actually believes it.

Phantoms

What are all these doing here?
Nerve splinters.
Pick them up with gloved fingers.
Flicker like heat lightning,
alive with messages.
Each one containing all of your life.
Why do you throw them away?
You are to examine the limits of the real,
and for this you will need them.

In the garden of wasps
you are a captive.
You have been signed away
by wife, doctor, employer.
In the isolation room for two and a half years,
your writing confiscated and used against you.
Name each one, name everything, parasitized by God.
And know the naming voice is nothing.

God's Tintinnabulation

Telepathy

Freud will think of me as gay,
and it is with a gay science
I greet this idea. He also
thinks I should have been made
professor of psychiatry and director
of a mental hospital. Well.
And all through the century of the telephone
they will discuss my primal scenes
as if there had not been so many others
looking for something on the other side
of pain and the looting repetitions of the known.
I carry the new name of the terrible disease,
and myself become one of the fleetingly improvised.
A hundred years from now it will seem
as if God had hung up on you.

Obituarying

It's Sunday and I wouldn't want to be too careful.
The sun's already awake and full.
The garden is filled with something
they would have called beauty
in the human language
which seems so far from me now.
To walk in the garden, azaleas,
rhododendrons, the gush of colour
they offer the world, the crepe
of petals, pollen tassels, as if
I weren't living a copy of my own life,
here, in this wicker chair,
its fraying nearly disguised
by a coat of white paint.

A copy of my own life,
in a fraying wicker chair,
disguised in white paint,
needles of white paint
that, when I turn my eyes to them,
sink into the skin without feeling,
as if my father were standing before me
in all his wrought-up agony, or
my brother
in his suicide shirt.

In his suicide shirt
there are brooks of blood
on his wedding day
gleaming into his nostrils,
slipping through his quicksilver eyes, uncured,
pooling in the palm of his left hand.
They follow the bullet's path,
rivuleting all the way to the well of the family name
where they tie themselves to our father's wrists, our father
who, in his last years never left the room
he wrote the famous books in
and drag him through his own opposites
like tides.

                 Each flooded with
others in the garden of the same.

The Chart

Has a tendency to want to get away (really!) *during a walk in the garden, inclines toward the lake, tries to jump out the window, at night, intermittent sleeping medicines, hallucinations so severe, becomes totally inaccessible, spends hours in the chair, afraid of molestation, believes* (believes!) *he is a girl.*

Often goes to the window and roars out (into the fibrillations of the rift of time) *returning to the conversation as if nothing had happened.* (Well?) *Says his body will begin to rot but his head will go on living* (surely a miracle!). *Writes in almost illegible letters* (personal things they are a screen for): (Save me from the unopened window).

The Appeal

What can definitively be said to be on the inside? Certainly not the soul.

This is my appeal. Words. Their frailty. Their multiple synapses. How they render things permeable. The botrytised fruit of them. When my life has become a ruined garden of noises, and soul murder is perpetrated. A mirror you look into and not see yourself. But the room and its hush of half-light, and the garden beyond, on fire with the rays of God, a bright gash in the world.

Flammenworte

Don't try this at home,
look at the cinders,
the words you can't listen to,
the moment you can't decide,
the open question, the
who-you-are question, questioned,
the speech the tongue
in humility can't recognize.
They burn up what they tell.
My nerves are trails of gunpowder,
rantings at the door.
They incinerated Europe
for a hundred years
and gouged a chimney
through the sky, still
visible today, the untold
souls fly up.
In the beginning was the emptiness of fire
calling out for things to devour.
And in the end, and
in the end,
what?
I don't know what you could say.

Judgements

Before the forecourts of heaven
I am arrayed,
my histories stream out
like shadows behind me,
ransacked with light,
the undersides of dreams.
Don't be fooled with diagnoses, I tell myself,
Freud will read me wrong,
Canetti confuse me with tyrants.
God is the sun, and wants to devour.
That is the sentence
which has nothing to do with madness.
And in God's language, the sentence
can never be completed.

The Acceleration of the Rays

Complete the Following

The thought of you there breaks
Beyond discipline is
Struck by
Is the sweep of petals against skin
Opening a tear in the
Inhalation of stars into my brain could
The terrible whispered smoke of
Might all the lost ones reside in
My manhood is
Why not
Live this body as
Memory wouldn't
Think of the rays as
The basic language says
But
If there were some way to get there
I would

Endless War

They would let fly and open up their narrowness
such that even the piano was often an object of their miracles.
I couldn't dream any louder trying to keep them at bay,
but no dreaming of any kind would be effective against them.
They spun out their instincts. And then
the attendants would lock me in the cell,
windowless and with stuffing for walls
and when they closed the door behind me
I thought I'd never see another morning
and lost all hope of ever greeting you again,
the clang of endless war
makes me long for the not-thinking-of-anything-thought,
the voluptuousness of rays spending themselves
in me, finally surrendering their imagoes of murder.

Oh, and Jung, he didn't want to have much to do with that reductionism, and he gave Freud the Totem, so it began. I like to think that I made a small contribution, but who, actually, gets cured? There is always more suffering than the world can embrace. It burns off in smoke everywhere. I myself believe in the oldest stories, their flying through the blood, Aredvi Sura Anahita still flowing from the sacred mountain to the sea in her voluptuous way, God needing us like food.

From the Distant World

The paths of the rays are more direct
than mere light, that bends and wants
to know something of objects. The rays
are God's object, there is for them
no inside, the rays piercing
into the room to slice off the heads
of the water iris, slicing into the innards
of the one lying in whiteness,
limning the fine filaments of nerves
and turning them into floating motes of dust
hot with contact and engraved with instruction.

To live for days.
Just days from them.

The big moth of the lungs, haemorrhaged, the
blood moth, oxygen moth, what is
dissolving, what rising up as if out of the grave?
In the territory of the voluptuous.
How the juicy body waters the desert of the mind.
Now as if something were coming back.
There is an outside not different from an inside,
taking in a deep breath of harrowed air.

The Outside

Whenever the outside flares at the limit
whenever the leaves of its trees glint and blind
whenever the locusts of the outside go underground
and take with them their shattering colours and mandibles, whenever
the loss of words wakens you, lying along its border
stretched out like a knife at the foot of the wall,
the knife that scratches away at the mortar around a few stones,
whenever you must ask what the outside is, with its brutal and free music,
and what is it that conducts the outside to you like shards of mica,
whenever you think it is the place you have lived, whenever
angels, fiery beings, a woman's fingers on your brow,
the impossible bliss of what looks into you
reveals itself by withdrawing, tearing the muscle off your bones,
whenever you remember what has not yet happened
even for a second, the shimmered world pierced through reflection,
light on the river beyond the wall just visible from a window
beckons, where the dead children escape their status and their names,
and you've gone inside out.

Sabine: Six Lost

The garden is ripe with fog.
What is wrong with me?
What is wrong with me?

The children come out of me
like small bloody animals,
breathless,
having left their hunger in me.

They are almost porcelain.
They are
almost....
And I would hold them with my hands
if they let me.

At the Persian Café

Blue

Why Persian Blue? Damselfly happiness
queen-of-the-forecourts-of-heaven blue,
walking-wounded-lightning blue,
iris-morning-glory blue
Yggdrasil indigo
or dreaded-Druid tree-woad,
carboniferous blue,
suzerain cerulean floating down
like thrown silk,
house-at-the-bottom-of-the-iceberg
                                    blue,
snow-shadow blue, the ruined
paradise,
                pourumarhka blue
darkened with death, livid
bruise, and then sky
over mountains over mountains over
mountains in the voluptuous haze
of the approaching distance, Farohar
sapphire of the summer of the soul
stooping, rapturing down
into the meadows of myriad eyes.

Punishment

Punishment is the house of gazes
hammered up against the not possible
of this new century, going over everything yet again
but worse, where there's something still missing
I'm elided into my loss of you.
Across the long wastes of the room
they are looking at me,
the nerves come undone
mylar sheath, synapse
dendrite rhizome of the true conversation,
thread of feeling, gossamer
plenitude broken, starved
of our bodies in the coming time, burned
the homes, scattered
through the valley of the mass grave,
shattered teeth, I want
to sleep for a thousand years, and dream,
and taste the grain of the Gods
under the storehouses of the great palaces.

The Passion

The very first moan is steeped in hungering
for the hymn of God, the her, the whore of the Sun,
raised, arrayed in damask of Persian blue, sky-y ripples,
a little fire of pomegranate twigs on the piano, this,
the end of the human, its limit
of longing, the Towers of Silence
carrying the dead upward, rushing into the sky,
into the heavy floating wings, the red naked
raid of the heads of vultures, it may be
a scream, miracled to break
past the boundaries, the borders
of what was thought
love, this sea
of sky, this sky-crashed boat.

If I told you I am the scattered one
they are trying to drive crazy,
if I told you I am under water in a corner
of the garden (lung), in a drawer
in the kitchen beside the helpless
knives (spleen), on the face
of the cursed clock in the long hall
to the library (hand), on the curled
cloud over slate roofs (eye),
in the fireplace by the ash grate (heart),
in the armoire with ivory inlay
animals (stomach), the excoriating
pain when my organs are pulled apart,
when my life is pulled asunder,
and the souls of the others plunge into me
like kingfishers into a river, their chatter,
the echo of my own fear,
fissured

Solitary

Sink. One tap. One bench with bedding. One
toilet. Single high horizontal
pipe. One grate.
One standing
for two and a half years
every night in the questioning place
fingers like spiders
skittering up the blind, fabricked walls
as if underground,
paralyzed, draped.
One stone floor.

One would hear
whimpering
but the voices
wouldn't hear completion.
Squirmed
with their tipped poison. One
is only
the outline of their attack.

Shadow room. No one's
room. One? No.
Rays pierce an eye
creating an iris for themselves,
and a looking.

Three Forensic Questions

Can it be maintained that there exists a morbid mental
derangement?

Like evaporation from stony ground
after a desert downpour,
like a library of books come to life
lifting off the pages,
the mind is a fiercely abstracted traveller
becoming the way.

Would liberty be a danger to himself or to others?

O blind knowledge that saves us from what?
The filigree nerve contact
as fine as the song of electricity running through things.

Is he incapable of looking after his own affairs?

You fling out Your minions
who clatter to the ground
like spent arrows. Trees spring up.
I walk with my daughter in the greening woods.

The Nerve Contact

Pitcher

I am conscious of how incredible this must seem to other human beings, but in spring the songbirds: finches, vireos; in summer, jays, swallows; and in winter, crows, were miracled with speech, which had been inscribed in them, and they would repeat what they had imbibed interminably, and because they worked on a scale of vibration, if I inserted, by thinking, a word of similar sound, they would stop their rote libation and pass over into the genuine feeling of delibility in an annihilation of chatter.

Don't forget all representing is nonsense; quicksilver might shine in the gleam of human being, say the house finches, which distinctly encourages me.

73

And these were everything I could contrive to take with me into the night of my cell. And they remain with me. And my heart was replaced with the ghost of a song, and my fingers with quills, the tiny open coffin of my name.

The Writing-Down-System

It occurs to me that I myself
am the writing-down-system
that wants to capture everything, even
the space between breaths,
the coffee stains on the white shirt cuff,
the diagonal sigh
of the bishop across the board,
the careless shrug of the shoulders,
the lingerie drawer half open, or three
quarters closed, the orange rind on the windowsill,
the scent of orange, the fingerprint
in the dust, the glance that finds
exactly what it's looking for,
but there is nothing here now but
pen and paper and darkness
they do not let me out of. I
cannot move, not even into the periphery
of dream. The darkness is lucid
with folds of satin, I cannot reply.
Freedom sustains itself
on limitation here, the endless
limitation of words I am writing
on the other side of writing.

The Institution of Writing

How will I keep hold of who I am,
                      negotiating (with) ghosts
in the Devil's Kitchen, here
                  in the dark of the cell
eating the glowing pomegranate
                    heart of grief
having been blasted by gods
                the nerve language
breaking cover and crackling over the floor
like a low sliding mist, a net of ankle-deep lightning
so filled with promise, so filled with pain
trickling up my body
             a braid of electricity
the intolerable suffering of this place accumulating
the heavy scent of hyacinth
             memory
a match dropped from the window into the night
                  well of breath
vertigo of the universe falling away?

Representing Questions

What can be more definite for a human being than what he has lived through and felt on his own body? But when someone says that he once used to be a drawing in a book, and only recently escaped to come here to the asylum, what can one say to that?

What if she had never existed and people only thought that she did?

Can each life really be one miracle after another?

Thought Experiment

Try this. *You are to be represented as...,* say the voices. Let's forget the *as* for the moment. Representation is always under the threat of substitution, but is not that, nor is it as far gone as doubling, nor as weak as *as if.* It's more like *giving an impression,* an overlay of difference. For instance, at the Dresden station I saw a fair number of people who gave the impression of being railway passengers.

A question along these lines of some import, given the malign forces afoot, might then be *If I am to be represented, to whom does such representing belong?*

Wall, Corridor, Balcony, Door

Up over
the garden wall
the huge rusty moon
slammed,
while the other one,
pale and white
at the apex of the sky,
stood ajar,
letting the most unhappy creatures
escape.
You might mistake them
for fireflies or stars.
You might see the shape
of the night.

You'd be
standing
on the balcony of drugs
unable to sleep.
Out in
the corridor, endless
war, keeping the walking
corpses in fear,
the hundreds hungering for the one
word and the one
who surely needs blaming.

Through your nostrils
you'd inhale stars
that when they reached the brain
would explode
nova thoughts with nowhere to go.

The teeming unending night,
so shaken by miracles

The Glistering of Female Nerves

The Forbidden Room

Nothing so necessary and allusive
as where we're not supposed to be,
always children of desire,
and the ripe smell of it
baking, reaching our nostrils
from the beginnings
carrying the names we were recipéed with
back into the locked cupboard of our selves.
Only when we're at the dining room table
may we handle the utensils
and only if we have behaved, no
striking, no bellowing, no
lunge of aggression, nothing
so rich and strange, the room
is a hoard of transformation devices,
devices of polished wood, bone,
mother-of-pearl, of shell, of silver
that press, cut, crush, mince,
measure, distill, boil, stir
braise, mix, fry, frappé, ferment
and serve, flights of knives, schools
of spoons, porcelain prides,
where the turnip invents
ingots of itself, the parsnip
is blessed with butter, the onion
releases its sharp soul, earth
rises up into fruit, jammed and jarred,
the peeled back petals of flesh, no matter
how curious, eager, patient and desperate we are
we are not permitted there, holding open
our heads like bowls, but when not locked down
like a wraith of the possible on a bat's wing I
nevertheless steal in

Exits and Entrances

Almost anything can be one. Typically wells and the mouths of caves, beside which one would have placed perhaps a flower or fruit. If I place my hand into the water of the sink the fingers disappear. None of the attendants notice this. But neither do they notice the lights folding like banners in the sky over the crumbling garden wall.

I am changed by water, though afraid of vanishing. I leave a jar of eau de vie, a toothbrush, and slip out from under the regulations. Currents quicken me.

School of red dart shiners ahead my skin reticulates into —shimmers, a sinew of instant delight, lines of pressure stripe wet blood, eddied forest of yellow bullheads, outdistancing the fingerlings, stepping out onto a shore where rocks seem to have just been born, rayed with fiery brightness, there is everything there is in the waking world, and everything is inside everything else, searching for what is lost.

A hill crawling with bright creatures suddenly darkens. Someone carrying a look, crying, over the river. A rope bridge, a paperweight in the drawer in the forest. The crumple of thunder.

Someone like an animal or a soul beckons me, but I'm afraid she may be a tested one. *Do not slake your thirst on me.* She points to where an opening gleams, like an eye of mica—shiny porcelain shoal surrounded by the shouting of attendants who want to claim me in the open blaze of the hopeless. *Leap, I will be their catch.*

The Exchanges

To one whose eyes leak tiny glances of heaven, I give
stainless utensils from the clutter of the kitchen, that pry
apart sky and earth in a brittle, shiny way to give her
breathing room. She gives me a pearl grey glove.

From another who needs a trowel from the garden shed
to plant the little flowers her visitors bring, a scarf filled
with the sipping of hummingbirds.

Mrs. Eberbach needs sweets, another gift from the trove-
room of the kitchen. Julie Boppard is a gambler with
whom I frequently play chess. The loser must surrender
something to the other, me a map of the underworld,
she a garter or shoe.

One needs the tiny bones and skulls of voles and the
other nearly always invisible mammals of the garden to
mark the boundary between useful and pointless time.
From her, an earring with stones like drops of blood.
And another needs the feather of a bee-eater to lure the
music of her childhood back.

Longing looms everywhere, the piano to be played,
the bed to be gardened, and if successfully resisted,
voluptuousness rises, and I'm a tree ablaze in the pouring
down of the rays.

The Passerby

The room with its arched door and deadbolt off the corridor
that leads to the library, could have walls
painted the green of new birch leaves.

Whoever walks past this room
is drawn toward it, hesitates before its door,
to look through the little peephole, that permits
only a view in one direction
or perhaps, is completely blind.

The room has exquisite patience, a gravity well,
adducing and absorbing into itself from the passersby
something of salt and pain and intimacy.
It does not open its windows
and its paintings, taken down, are covered in white linen.
It has a name, but can't remember it.
                              In the room,
perhaps music has been played, piano and cello. O
the books once read!
                    Into the walls
as if into a forest, the sounds of the turning pages,
of the music, of your voice, at once clear and muted,
the characters coming to life, enacting the passion
of the others, being momentarily amazed with this
so-called life.

One, Crossing

the river in a rowboat
pulling oneself hand over hand
by rope in the dusk
arrives just behind oneself

Water rises to the feet of the columns
of the forecourts of heaven
as one steps ashore

A little breeze lifts the leaves
of the acanthus on the left
like a skirt

What's left of the day's light
is drawn into the things it had touched
leaving only a faint residue of visibility
like a memory of the things themselves

In the stillness, the hush at the nearly stopped moment:
one is looking for the lost ones
the children who refused to slip into bodies
crying *not yet not yet*
abandoning longing before it could begin

The braided before and after
touching smelling each other
wisteria whale song light
licked off the faces of loved ones
and the one who carries such love

By the windows of keyholes
by the eyes of birds
by the bead of blood
by the dark drops of apple seed
and the mica gleam of salmon scale
by the notes hung on gibbets of air
flung out like smashed sweat, by the
ember of heart
banked under the tear in the earth
by the sisters whose ears refused the drink of words
by the mother who polished the skies
by the spirit whisper of pine woods
the broken slash of mirror
in the wrist of the river
by the sieved pearl of the split second
by the water table of truth
in the asylum library
slipping through the you and the I
smooth, adamant, archaic, aflame

Nearing the Home Near the Woods

Sabine: Accommodation

We come at last to the cool breezes
just on the far side of hurt
as if we'd walked into a grove
of young birch from the unbearable
heat of the meadow.

Were you following a sacred thread
I could not leave for you?
I remember your face
as you walked through those gates.
How did I look?

I had not known all these years
what to do, waiting, waiting
with almost nothing to wait for, afraid to hope
afraid mostly, of you, for you,
the unbearable eruptions of shouting,
screams at night, the long unmovable
stares, eyes an empty sky,
language that breaks, breaks
things, and ravels in all directions.

The new house you will build for us
has been waiting, waiting, your new
daughter I could not tell you of.

In the dream there is such weeping, the brushfires
of war sweeping across the world
under the paved cities by rays of roots
over rivers in towers of orange lightning
and in the aftermath smolderings
I come upon, like an archaeologist,
the remnant of the human language
I'd almost forgotten had existed, Sabine,
like a ring lost long ago in another life,
a pale yellow glint among ashes.

Seedlings

Things that nest in (replace) me:

field mice, golden finches, ganglia,
broken shards
of souls that have been blown out the windows
or fallen into the wells, sharp-
eared owls, vowels and consonants
that are yet to come,
a family on a picnic by the sea,
towering clouds, lipstick,
the moment of the backward glance,
how they look at me in the shining field of the mirror
under the towering cloud, the cradle of the eye,
irradiating the careless child
caressed by a distant hand
who forgot his scarf at school
and whose heartbeat is the discipline of suffering, who is
yanked out of bed at night
so the dream is stranded and yearns
to be dreamed again,
the child who falls through space
his whole life afterward this downward arc
the family built over the ache of falling:
the searing edge of the caress,
the tendrilling ache of the everyday.

Heartwood

The first succulence rises
where, like a dream of dishes crashing
from shelves, the door is flung open
onto a garden, jittered with virid light
just under the skin,
and it is fear and desire at once,
but has no name
because sapblood floods me,
and I am a mouth He longs for
filling me with incessance,
just within the work of the dream gliding
towards its forsakeness in the silver
and porcelain morning mist,
quincebloom and melon hued, crossing
over here and here and here, just where
something has gone into the green depths of the pond
burnished ripples arise repeatedly revealing
the secret happiness of disappearance.

Mercy

There are those who believe
that weeds are the interregnum
of order. There are those who believe
that poetry and jokes have a natural affinity,
and that writing carries
a writer's name.

My hands
                    now with serpents
just beneath the skin
        flowing over bone.

I climb into the hull of my bed.
I begin to practice penmanship.

These days my confession is with cardinals
bee-eaters, or tits, those listening by casting
their sultry brightness abroad, with
these woods at the edge of the house.

I would like to die,
when that time comes,
not in an institution:
such catalogues of humiliation
and interpretation
that have parsed me without mercy
far from the ones I love.

Let me be light
                    as a milkweed seed
        drifting
over garden walls.

The Reverie

The long clinamen of commentary
reaching backward to an unclaimable origin
where what happened to us we did not experience
and waits to occur. The still-to-come. The verb
to be. The unlocking of the gates,
and the throwing away of the key.
Cloud break at sunset
smudging your skin with darkening
ruddy-gold light,
and all along the edge of evening, your looking
that is my language, unravelling me—
which is not an image, but the space beyond it
vastly emptied, a reverie
that has yet to wash over us.

The Content of Saturation

Waves/Particles

This scatter
                    how the bed of the stream is
stones   twigs   sunken leaves   reeds   sunken
glints of sunlight
                              lying at the bottom of the
darkened
        cell   the body throws off
emanations   photo-
graphs   something
                              carried   down-
stream
        the child at the table
with apparatus
                              sitting oh so straight
the courtroom appearance in suit
the Easter Sunday of sullen heat
girl with her legs outstretched and eyes closed
flying on the swing
                              the father
cascading down steps
the amplitude of memory
                              long skeins of silt
drifting
        drifting downstream

The morning-glory-blue shimmer of listening
Ear of the earth hearing
The drinking-in of the unsounded
Just across the memory river,
The tongue of the hummingbird
Evangelizing the hurricanes of nectar,
Of which your word-night is the eye,
You
The portage of blood.

For My Mother

The deranged heads of the hydrangea
peonies dropping scented petals
to the floor, the prisoner
hooded, shackled
to the doorway for days.

I don't recognize you in the casket
the warmth of you drained away.
Everyone trying to identify their dead
in the new wars, claim the unclaimable.

Purple beech leaves polished by wind, by sun.

You, having given
yourself away,

Ein Bahn Reise

Haunted stations, we clatter
In silence
Ghosts
Of all those
Who have travelled by train
Through dark *Wald* and field, past
Infinitely
Tidy *Schrebergärten*, and
Towns of medieval charm
Are listening
Slipped through the chink, and
Accumulated
The destination
Adjacent to mourning

Crossing

If you do this properly, you will be able to cross the boundary
of death at will, the holy one seeing into the mind of the king.
Do you mean reading or telling? asked the king.

I noticed for the first time that we were seated in the shade
of a tamarind tree. That attendants brought tray
after tray of heavenly food beginning with fruit:
sliced papaya and pitted mango, guavas
and bananas, sweet oranges and sugarcane,

and I looked down into the coffin
you were not buried in because
you were burned in the fire
and scattered into water with my own hand,
but your body was rotting there, disintegrating like rags,
and I was addicted to several painkillers.

On the boundary, behind a cluster of tall reeds
I noticed several young courtesans who were splashing in the water,
painted with red and golden oils that streaked down their faces,
seedheads of the tall grasses like fireworks
exploding without moving, not thinking of
the refugees in possession of nothing
but their own unhappiness.

Well, we're fucked here then, between worlds of splendour.
Stay out of the crystal pavilion, she'd said then,
*it holds a pool that leads to the world of humans,
if you fall in there you shall not be able to return.*

Little Throats

He would blow on my body
until brains slid out the pores
in the reek of unwashed sheets
each with the name of a swan.
Come closer my little ones
arrive at me   only one limit
of a freedom you can almost
imagine the outside of.
Do not think of history as the already
written   the reports of the doctors.
The *Memoirs* were counterproof
and had to be meticulous
caution governed me.
Will you find me on the far
side of power   little poems
holding out your hands
as if you were blind
make me still   little throats

Notes

PERHAPS, DEAR READER, you will be familiar with *Memoirs of My Nervous Illness with Appendices and an Addendum About the Question, "Under what circumstances can a person considered insane be detained in an asylum against his will?"* published in the year after my freedom, 1903, which began a cascade of scribbling throughout the century from the likes of Freud, Jung and Bleuler, to Canetti, Niederland, Lacan, Deleuze and Anthony Wilden, not to mention many others less famous. Beginning with Freud in 1911, who had been busy suppressing longings for his colleague Fliess in the wake of the dissolution of that friendship. In fact, almost at the exact moment Freud and Fliess were discussing the unconscious for the first time, I was deprived of my freedom in Dresden, halfway between Fliess's Berlin and Freud's Vienna. That would have been in 1895.

Now surely these *Denkwürdigkeiten* are enough for everyone, at least for everyone to use as evidence—even *too* much, overwrought with systemizing, overwritten with an eye to impossible proof, and appended documents: medical reports, hospital charts (in the new translations); it does not give way on principle, but I must now confess it is not all I wrote during those terrible years of my confinement, and what your eyes now witness, is something quite different, something I had hidden away from the guards, the doctors, and the others.

Although many keys carried across to the other side, such as you will find in *Voluptuousness is a state of mind*, naturally occur in both, writing the *Memoirs* would enable my freedom, the writing of these, the release of something else.

Against the crenellating, the constant rustling of the voices, against the forensic languages and official pronouncements, the forking lightning of the nerve language and how a human being in many places at once might learn to listen.

PHANTOM MIND

Completion. Voices demand. Demand the sentences they begin be completed. That I complete them. Those that arise out of the fissure are outside God's realm and cannot be sustained. They are my coat turned inside out, the hairs on my head turned white, whatever flickers and wavers in the corner-of-the-eye-effect, whatever hesitates before the light, and stepping into it, become sheer, nearly looked through, speaking the words that existed before the existence of the world.

SELF PORTRAIT WITH NERVES

Because that's what we readers do. Judge Schreber and the slightly overshooting blood metallic tinsel oxide smell of success, Senatspräsident of the Supreme Court of the State of Saxony. Saxophony. Rumi, my roomy. God's impossible. Language. Nervous knell.

THE HOUSE SAILING

It was as if a single night had the duration of centuries, so that within that time period the most profound alterations in the whole of humankind, in the earth itself and the whole solar system could very well have taken place.

THE MIRACLE OF UNMANNING

Sabine, my wife, my dearest, *flütige hingemacht.*

SPARTA OF CHILDHOOD

In 1842 I was born in the dust under the angel of summer, Daniel Paul Schreber. Incipient things like names take you. And *die Nadel.* You can possibly imagine. Why would the quite famous father (who was an outdoors name, a name after the Greeks and gymnasia, "Learning the art of renouncing on the lap of the mother," and "repeated physically perceptible admonitions" to make the Germans Greek, disaster of the imaginary belonging) be longing?

Innocence Is the Weakest Defence
The title of this piece has been written by a future prisoner, Mr. Leonard Pelltier.

Something Terrible Has Happened
such that the flame is mutagenic, as in 1945 and 2045, the angel of history looks away, where somewhere I went wrong.

Sabine
who was gone. Who needed my money. To Switzerland. Arranged by her repellent father, some musical snob, and whom did she meet there? Under sheets of Alpine snow. Under guard, under lock and key, under duress, I'm thinking of her.

Tincture of Necrin
impossible neuroleptic. Because often everything though just the same on the outside can release the smell of iron in the air that can tell you in fact the inside has been totally replaced with alien substances and chemistries and only then can you ask what freedom is.

Reading Thoughts
Books *or* other notes *are kept in which for years have been* written down *all my thoughts, all my phrases, all my necessaries, all the articles in my possession or around me, all the persons with whom I come into contact, etc.* And I must find a way through this system.

Searching for the Golden Drop
First cataclysm healed at 42, second in 1893 at 52, after my promotion, not so lucky. Voluntarily at first, disappeared into the asylum for nine years, solitary, *die Nadel,* Doctors Flechsig and Weber who argued for my continual incarceration; disappeared in a metonymy of soul murders, into the rift in the soul of the world. All the disappeared.

Seelenpolitik
Sabine's excursions to Switzerland could have produced an anxious moment, a toil, a miracle. The truth has a hand in me. She will remember me fondly when there are only miracles, tombs, nothing to eat. Realpolitik.

Representations
The house of the forsaken. To open the drawer is beyond voices, the secret bridge on the tip of the tongue. On the inside you find out you are no longer free, realize what you have never been

free from. What begins and returns is never complete. What is complete will lie, given the chance. What I know and can speak of, the writing-down-system wrests from me. And the world must be represented or the world will disappear. I will be a filled drawer.

PICTURING

The doctors can't grasp the importance of this. Picturing throws out beings into the world, male and female, while I am at pains not to appear to

PHANTOMS

And the nature of this God, capricious, even at times malevolent, perhaps filled with distain, but with always an interest in sparrows, an interest in the limits of the human, with a love that makes us all ghosts.

TELEPATHY

Like omega beta waves, fragmented chirr-drones along the edge of consciousness, electronic GPS songlines, an old Harper era eugenics clinic, the stumble through bone dust all around us the mutant birch sheathed in copper paper like the heat from the ovens, the omens of grass ghost writing on the blue lapis welter of sky, like a tenuous projectile of thought bursting out the back of your skull, like telling you another story, we are here just for this moment of consternation, and what needed to be said, and what answered.

OBITUARYING

My father, Daniel Gottlieb Moritz Schreber, who fell from a ladder into a ten year depression and into the whole stretch of the nineteenth century, and in an underground way even today in Germany, trailing a substantial influence as a champion of strict moral upbringing, family values, hygiene and physical exercise, and my syphilitic brother who suicided two days before his wedding, would however be impeccable in death.

FLAMMENWORTE

Who would imagine Luther, who needed words to be flames and whose words inflamed, would still be wanted against human tinder.

JUDGEMENTS
Canetti, in *Crowds and Power*, will align paranoiacs with poets (without meaning to) by writing, "The most marked trend in paranoia is that towards a complete seizing of the world through words."

Freud will say, "It remains for the future to decide whether there is more delusion in my theory than I should like to admit, or whether there is more truth in Schreber's delusion than other people are as yet prepared to believe."

Yes.

OH, AND JUNG
Flowing through here, a replica of the world, a Persian river, a goddess of fertility, the souls of the sick.

BLUE
"Pourumarhka" is a Persian term used by Zarathustra to mean "filled with death," and the falcon with the ring of soul is grace, when Mithra's rays fertilize the earth, and like Nietzsche, I am Persian.

PUNISHMENT
The coming time that already will have happened, the anatomy of rivalry the doctors will brook, father's *Geradehalter*, severed heads and hands.

Hope, such a frail human thing, a person, an open, written, twisted one, the listening that is far from home, the I Who am distant.

SOLITARY
Die Nadel

THREE FORENSIC QUESTIONS
The Law, when God is master of corpses—I carry it, though it is not mine, I am quick (but with immeasurable effort) to use it, since it used me, I find it has fears, and the names of the mothers haunt it.

THE WRITING-DOWN-SYSTEM
Not to mention "uncanny particularity" according to Louis A. Sass.

THOUGHT EXPERIMENT
The problem with the voices: (has to be completed)

WALL, CORRIDOR, BALCONY, DOOR
I was billeted in the female wing for some months, hearing the voices of the others on the way to the cells.

EXITS AND ENTRANCES
Entranced tested souls filamentingly tying-to-celestial-bodies.

THE PASSERBY
What I call "so-called" is called so by the voices. Now wasn't that easy?

ONE, CROSSING
I know there must be other ways of writing these things, but now, it's as if you had been and I'm undone. Not nearly so easy.

BY THE WINDOWS OF KEYHOLES
the whole braided order of the world appears as a miraculous structure, capable of complete transformation while remaining the same, which I have to learn over and over again so painfully. I might be (painfully) reminded of *Babylon Babies,* where schizos are the next stage of evolution, however, Narby will write of *Intelligence in Nature*. Picture it.

SABINE: ACCOMMODATION
Sabine is 15 years younger than me. I married her in 1878. Fridoline, though perhaps a daughter by another while I was lost, will yet find me, and in interviews will say so.

SEEDLINGS
The terror bombs will have come, whistling or soundless, will be coming, arising from desperate need, the mind wanders backward and forward over the waste landscape of time with its weeds and everything, sniffing like a dog. The mind opens like an iris. The body's (s)trumpet vine.

WAVES/PARTICLES
Kabbalah says in the wake of the withdrawal of God: the ache of creation, during which it is our task to knit the scattered light.

THE MORNING-GLORY-BLUE
the spent flower's volute has sung with red.

FOR MY MOTHER

And then? *To create a human being an extraordinary exertion of power is necessary perhaps even incompatible with the very existence of God.*

My mother has died. Memory. *Mutterteil.* The torque of the vulnerable.

In six months Sabina will have a stroke. And the house I built, and my daughter, and, are, and not, and no protection, enough, unseeable, unsayable, unsoothable, unsuitable. Come back.

Never to, *the running out of the clocks of the world.*

Reinstitutionalized 1907. (Dead 1911.) Drops of rainwater on sun-warmed stone

EIN BAHN REISE

Herded "passengers" unheard. The terrible destinations from these platforms. The beautiful little gardens on the outskirts human beings could tend. Gone forward a little again, only to come back.

CROSSING

I must have been *Climbing Chamundi Hill* with Ariel Glucklich. The soul is indeed a traveller.

Acknowledgements

My thanks to the editors of *Rampike, stonestone, The Antigonish Review* and *The Windsor Review* who were kind enough to publish earlier versions of some of the poems. Such support is much appreciated.

The book would not have the shape that it does if it weren't for the editorial intuition and expertise of Don McKay. I am grateful for his inspired interventions.

Finally, I thank Charlene (without whom there is no word) for her response to the developing manuscript, and for her love.

BRIAN HENDERSON is the author of nine collections of poetry, including a deck of visual poem-cards, *The Alphamiricon*. He has published articles, reviews, and poetry in many literary magazines such as *Arc*, *Antigonish Review*, *Canadian Forum*, *Canadian Literature*, *CVII*, *Descant*, *ECW*, *The Fiddlehead*, *Prism*, *Quarry*, *Rampike*, *Rune* (of which he was a founding editor for its decade of existence), *Scrivener*, *The Windsor Review* and *Writ*. He's a photographer, has been a drummer in a rock band, and an occasional teacher. He has a PhD in Canadian literature and is the director of Wilfrid Laurier University Press. He lives with the love of his life, his son, step-son, a frequently visiting daughter, and a relentlessly curious dog. There is only a little madness in the family.